Careers with Animals

Veterinarian

Trudi Strain Trueit

Cavendish Square
New York

Published in 2014 by Cavendish Square Publishing, LLC
303 Park Avenue South, Suite 1247, New York, NY 10010

Copyright © 2014 by Cavendish Square Publishing, LLC

First Edition

Website: cavendishsq.com

This publication represents the opinions and views of the author based on his or her personal experience, knowledge, and research. The information in this book serves as a general guide only. The author and publisher have used their best efforts in preparing this book and disclaim liability rising directly or indirectly from the use and application of this book.

CPSIA Compliance Information: Batch #WW14CSQ

All websites were available and accurate when this book was sent to press.

Library of Congress Cataloging-in-Publication Data

Trueit, Trudi Strain.
Veterinarian / by Trudi Strain Trueit.
p. cm. — (Careers with animals)
Includes index.
ISBN 978-1-62712-464-5 (hardcover) ISBN 978-1-62712-465-2 (paperback) ISBN 978-1-62712-466-9 (ebook)
1. Veterinarians — Juvenile literature. 2. Veterinary medicine — Vocational guidance — Juvenile literature. I. Trueit, Trudi Strain. II. Title.
SF756.T78 2014
636.089—dc23

Editorial Director: Dean Miller
Senior Editor: Peter Mavrikis
Copy Editor: Cynthia Roby
Art Director: Jeffrey Talbot
Designer: Amy Greenan
Photo Researcher: Julie Alissi, J8 Media
Production Manager: Jennifer Ryder-Talbot
Production Editor: Andrew Coddington

Printed in the United States of America

CONTENTS

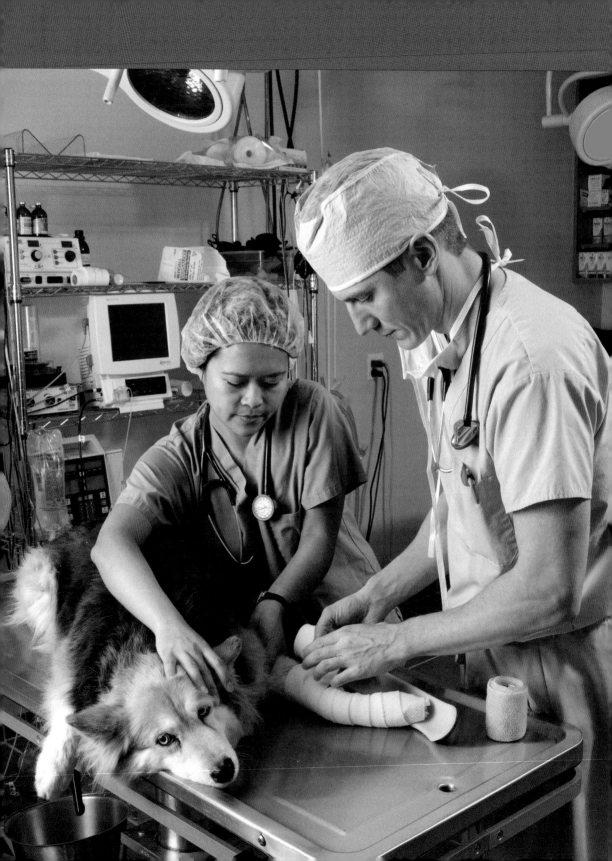

ONE

A Heart for Animals

D r. Christie Carlo is having a busy day. It started with an emergency. A dog that had eaten fifteen antacid tablets, some dark chocolate, and a protein bar was rushed into her Des Moines, Iowa, veterinary hospital. Chocolate and medications intended for humans can be fatal to **canines**. Soon after, another dog was brought in with an injured toe.

He was taken for X-rays to check for fractures while Dr. Carlo and her colleagues determined that their first patient hadn't eaten enough of the harmful substances to be hospitalized. With the ruckus from the emergencies finally settling, Dr. Carlo is able to get to her regularly scheduled appointments. "It's not surprising," she says with a laugh, "just exciting."

For veterinarians like Dr. Carlo, the job can be challenging and the days full. Working with ill and injured animals, and their worried owners, takes a cool head.

But most veterinarians thrive on such pressure. They are not easily deterred. They have already been down a long and difficult road to get to this point in their lives.

Many veterinarians have known what they wanted as a career since they were children. Most started working with animals besides their own pets when they were in middle school or even elementary school. They may have

(Opposite) A veterinarian's day is full with treating injured animals, surgery, and routine exams.

volunteered at a veterinary office, animal shelter, **wildlife sanctuary**, or kennel—anywhere they could gain experience with animals. It's also likely they went to an animal-oriented summer camp, joined 4-H Youth Development or Future Farmers of America, and got involved in science and math clubs at school. Their journey has taken them through three to four years of **undergraduate** courses at a university, followed by four years of veterinary school. After graduation from veterinary school, they may have continued their studies by becoming board certified in a specialty area, such as surgery, emergency medicine, or canine and **feline** practice. This required a one-year **internship** followed by a **residency**, two to three years of learning under the supervision of a qualified veterinarian. Why did they work so hard? Veterinarians love learning. They love a fast-paced life. Most of all, they love helping animals.

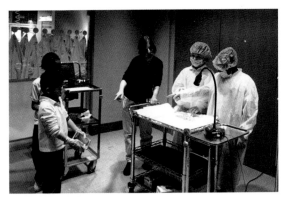

Animal Adventures

At the Santa Fe Animal Shelter's annual Critter Camp in New Mexico, kids get the inside scoop on what it's like to have a career working with animals. Designed for students aged nine to twelve, the summer camp teaches about basic veterinary care and animal welfare issues. Campers can also work in a satellite clinic and even help animals recover from **anesthesia**. Numerous shelters, Humane Society branches, and zoos across the country offer similar camps. To find one near you, contact your local zoo or animal shelter, or check out your state's Humane Society website.

People have been treating and caring for animals for hundreds of years. This painting from 1390 depicts the mending of a horse's leg.

A Passion for Healing

For as long as animals and people have shared Earth, it seems that people have looked after the health of the creatures in their care. Some of the earliest known records detailing the practice of veterinary medicine date back nearly four thousand years. The Kahun Papyri, a collection of Egyptian medical writings, contains pieces of a veterinary papyrus. The hieroglyphs detail animal **anatomy**, diseases, and treatments. Similar evidence from Greece, China, India, and the Americas show other early civilizations also provided medical care for their animals. In the first century AD, a Roman scholar and animal-care expert named Columella wrote at length about the breeding and health care of **livestock**. He coined the term *veterinarius* to describe someone who took care of pigs, cattle, and sheep. It comes from the Latin word *veterinum*, which means "beast of burden." This is how we came to call animal doctors veterinarians.

Today, the United States is home to more than 90,000 licensed veterinarians. Most, like Dr. Carlo, are in private practice. They may have a clinic of their own or share one with several other doctors. Private practice veterinarians typically select one area of medicine. They may treat companion animals (dogs and cats), exotic pets (rabbits, birds, reptiles, rodents, wildlife), equines (horses), or large animals (cows, sheep, llamas). Some doctors have a combined practice. A veterinarian's job is to treat animals that are ill and injured, as well as to educate owners on how to properly care for them.

(opposite) Many veterinarians work in a private practice. They choose one area to specialize in, such as companion animals.

Should You Be a Veterinarian?

- Do you love helping animals?
- Can you handle seeing animals hurt or ill?
- Do you like dealing with people?
- Can you work well under pressure in a hectic environment?
- Do you have the patience to solve challenging problems?
- Do you enjoy your academic classes, particularly in science, math, and English, and can you earn top grades in them?
- Are you willing to go to school for four more years after completing college, plus continue to do periodic training once you are a veterinarian?

If you answered "yes" to all of these questions, veterinary medicine could be a good career choice for you.

Many other opportunities exist in veterinary medicine beyond private practice. Thousands of zoos, aquariums, shelters, and wildlife sanctuaries across the nation employ veterinarians. Some animal doctors work for the government, caring for dogs used in the military or for homeland security. Others are dedicated to protecting public health. They inspect animals coming into the country or those bound for the food supply. Veterinarians are instrumental in studying and managing the spread of zoonotic diseases, illnesses that can be passed from animals to humans. Those who go into research are often on the cutting edge of new drug, vaccine, surgical technique, and medical discoveries. Some veterinarians have an eye on the future and teach their craft to a new generation of animal doctors at veterinary schools.

The veterinary profession is demanding, but the rewards are great. An immense pride comes from healing animals, advising pet owners, and working for the public good. Whether studying the tiniest microbe or tending the largest whale, veterinarians can take satisfaction in knowing they are making a difference in the world.

TWO

The Road to a Dream

A desire to improve the lives of animals and humans is a good basis for a career in veterinary medicine. But it is only the first step of many. Becoming a veterinarian is a goal that takes careful preparation, and the earlier you start, the better.

If you are planning a career in veterinary medicine, you should take college-preparatory classes in science, math, and English in middle school and high school. (Take honors, advanced placement, or the highest level you can achieve.) Science coursework should include biology, chemistry, and physics. Take zoology and anatomy and physiology if your high school offers them. In math, take algebra, geometry, calculus, and statistics. An English curriculum should include composition and literature. You should also take a foreign language, computer courses to learn software applications and web design, speech or drama to improve your communication proficiency, and business classes to help you understand money management, if you have access to them. These are all skills required to run a successful veterinary practice. Academic counselors say it's also important not to get so focused on science and math that you forget to become well-rounded or to develop interests outside of veterinary medicine. They suggest taking courses in art, music, and social studies, too. Maintaining a 3.0 (B) gradepoint average (GPA) or higher in high school is recommended. Those with top grades have an edge when applying to college and veterinary school.

A high school course of study that includes science classes is recommended for students who would like a career in veterinary medicine.

Outside of the classroom, you should join clubs that revolve around science and math, leadership, and speech. Become active in 4-H, Future Farmers of America, Pony Club, or a pre-veterinary club. In addition, getting hands-on experience working with animals in middle school and high school is highly recommended. Veterinary school applications will ask how much time you have spent working with animals. They will also request that you provide letters of recommendation from college professors and professionals you have worked with in the past. That's why it's important to not only gain experience but also to make a good impression on the people who supervise you. A local veterinarian's office, kennel, shelter, farm, zoo, or wildlife sanctuary is a great place to volunteer. Always keep a written journal of activities you performed, and log the number of hours you worked. Some veterinary schools want applicants to have 1,000 hours of experience working with animals, which amounts to two to three summers of full-time work. (These hours can be obtained throughout the school year as well.)

The Undergraduate Experience

Graduating with a degree in veterinary medicine is a two-step process. The first step is to take undergraduate courses at a private or public university. We'll get to which courses to take in a moment. The second step is to choose a veterinary school to go to once your undergraduate curriculum is complete. With this career field, though, you need to be thinking about the second step first. That's because every veterinary school has its own set of prerequisites, or classes students are required to take before applying. So before choosing an undergraduate college or university, you must determine the veterinary schools to which you want to apply. (You can apply to more than one school at a time.)

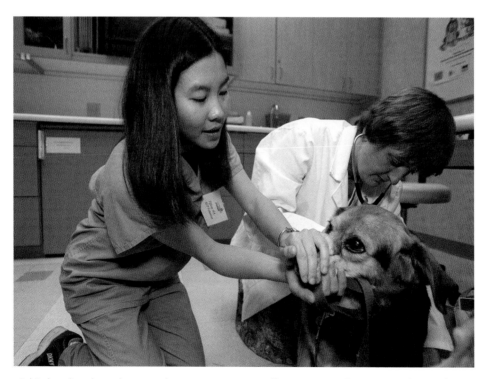

A high school student works at a veterinary office as part of an internship to learn about a career in veterinary medicine.

There are twenty-eight accredited veterinary colleges in the United States, five in Canada, and eleven in foreign countries that meet the American Veterinary Medical Association's (AVMA) standards of excellence. For a complete list of veterinary schools and links to their prerequisites, visit the Association of American Veterinary Medical Colleges' (AAVMC) website.

Although each veterinary college has its own set of prerequisites, most have similar lists. Here are the prerequisites from the College of Veterinary Medicine at Iowa State University, which total sixty credit hours.

- General chemistry (one year)
- Organic chemistry (one year)
- Biochemistry (one semester)
- General biology (one year)
- Genetics (one semester)
- Anatomy or physiology (one semester)
- General physics (one semester)
- English composition (one year)
- Oral communication (one semester)
- Humanities and social studies (one year)
- Electives (one year)

Prerequisites usually take two to three years to complete. Most veterinary schools require applicants to have a GPA of 3.0 or above. Again, the higher the GPA, the better.

Once you have narrowed the field and have a couple of veterinary schools in mind, it's time to go back to step one and choose where to study at the undergraduate level. Most public and private universities in the United States offer all veterinary school prerequisites. Some may offer more classes in the areas you are interested in, as well as more opportunities to work with animals. Consider doing your undergraduate work in the same state in which you hope to go to veterinary school. This will give you an advantage. Veterinary schools select more in-state than out-of-state applicants. Also, tuition for in-state veterinary students is often much less expensive than it is for those from out of state.

On completing the prerequisites, you may apply to veterinary school. However, because the competition to get into veterinary school is steep, many academic advisors recommend that you go the extra year (or two) to earn an undergraduate degree, or bachelor's degree. A bachelor's degree takes about four years to complete. It is earned by taking specific courses

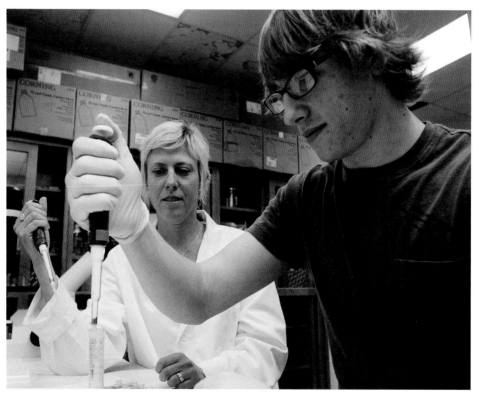

Students at the University of Florida research sea horse breeding in captivity. Studies such as this at the undergraduate level may help when applying to veterinary school.

in one area of study, called a major. Most veterinary schools do not direct students to choose a particular major. Any major is acceptable, as long as you meet the prerequisites and your science grades are strong. Many veterinarians say they majored in animal sciences, zoology, or biology, but others chose engineering, computer science, and even communication arts. The AVMA says the most important thing is to pick a major that you will enjoy and can excel in.

After you complete the prerequisites or earn a bachelor's degree, you must take a standardized written admissions test for veterinary school. All

If the School Fits...

When choosing your undergraduate school, be sure to do your homework. Look for a university that offers all of your veterinary prerequisites, along with a solid program in the area in which you want to major. Here are some questions to ask academic advisors.

• How successful are students from this school at being admitted to veterinary school?

• Do advisors take an active role in helping students plan for application to veterinary school?

• Does the campus have any facilities where I can get hands-on experience working with animals?

• Does your school have a pre-veterinary club, newsletter, or other activities that will allow me to connect with students who have interests similar to mine?

veterinary schools in the United States require applicants to take either the Graduate Record Examination (GRE) or the Medical College Admission Test (MCAT).

Now it is time to apply to veterinary school. You will apply to one or more veterinary schools online through the Veterinary Medical College Application Service, or VMCAS (an arm of the AAVMC). On your application, you will include your work experience and write a personal statement—an essay about why you want to become a veterinarian. Your undergraduate grades, GRE or MCAT test scores, and three letters of recommendation also get submitted. The letters typically are written by college professors, veterinarians, or professionals you have worked with to gain experience in the field. The VMCAS accepts applications from June to October of each year. The processing service then sends them on to the appropriate schools for review.

Each veterinary school has its own application review committee. At UC Davis School of Veterinary Medicine, applicants are evaluated on several things. Half of the ranking is determined by academics (grades from undergraduate school and admissions test scores). Thirty percent is determined by nonacademic factors, including letters of recommendation, a personal essay, and experience with animals. The final 20 percent is based on a face-to-face interview. Many veterinary schools in the United States follow a similar candidate review process. The competition to get into veterinary college is stiff. According to the AAVMC, less than half of those who apply are accepted.

Welcome to Veterinary School

For those fortunate enough to be accepted into veterinary school, it is the beginning of a new and busy chapter in their lives. Students spend four years studying to earn a veterinary degree, or doctor of veterinary medicine (DVM). Veterinary school teaches students the skills they need to provide health care for most types of animals. The broad curriculum covers surgery,

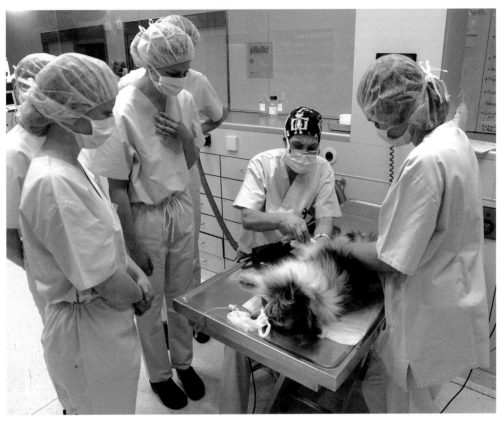

These veterinary students perform a mock surgery as part of their studies.

emergency care, anesthesia, diagnostic imaging (X-rays, CT scans), nutrition, dental health, eye care, pain management, rehabilitation, aging, and more.

Most veterinary schools in the United States also run teaching hospitals. This allows students to put what they are learning into practice and gain hands-on skills. When students are in the third or fourth year of veterinary school, they will start working with staff veterinarians at the school's hospital, examining patients, giving vaccinations, and assisting with surgeries. Staff and student veterinarians at the Cornell University Hospital for Animals in Ithaca, New York, treat more than 60,000 patients a year, from dogs to horses to eagles.

A veterinary student at the UC Davis Veterinary Medical Teaching Hospital makes notes about his patient after an examination.

The High Price of a Goal

The AAVMC reports that the average cost of attending four years of veterinary school in the United States runs between $155,000 and $240,000 (this includes books, fees, health insurance, housing, and other living expenses). Students who travel from another state to attend school may pay up to 50 percent more for their tuition than those who live in state. Financial assistance is available through loans, work-study programs, and scholarship programs. The AVMA, the American Kennel Club, and the U.S. Department of Health and Human Services are some of the organizations that offer scholarships.

Students in their fourth year of veterinary school are required to complete one or more **externships**. These programs are designed to give students real-world experience in veterinary medicine. Externships typically last from three to eight weeks. During the program, students work alongside professional veterinarians on the job. SeaWorld, the Smithsonian National Zoological Park, the Wildlife Conservation Society, and the U.S. Department of Agriculture are among the businesses that offer veterinary externships.

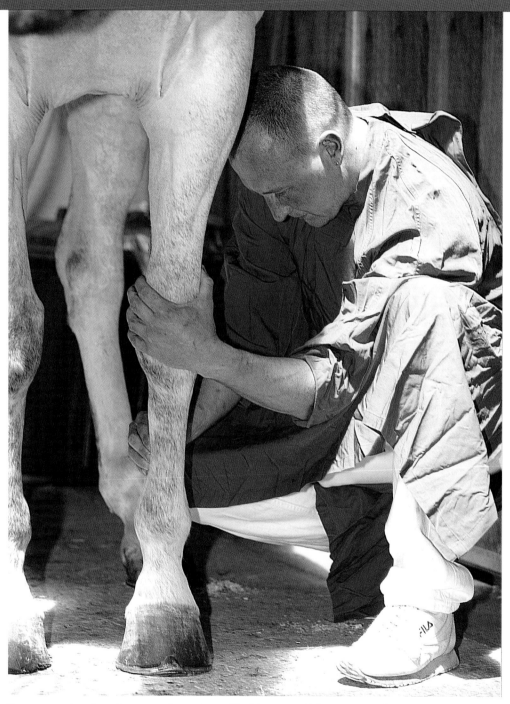

Some veterinarians become board certified in a specialty area, such as equine.

Congratulations, Graduates

Each year, about 2,700 veterinary students in the United States receive their DVM degree. At the commencement ceremonies, students in the graduating class stand before their friends and families to recite the Veterinarians' Oath:

Being admitted to the profession of veterinary medicine,
I solemnly swear to use my scientific knowledge and skills for
the benefit of society through the protection of animal health
and welfare, the prevention and relief of animal suffering,
the conservation of animal resources, the promotion of public
health, and the advancement of medical knowledge.
I will practice conscientiously, with dignity, and in keeping
with the principles of veterinary medical ethics.
I accept as a lifelong obligation the continual improvement
of my professional knowledge and competence.

Graduates must do one final thing before they can practice medicine—get a license. Veterinarian licensing is overseen by a governing board in each of the fifty states and the District of Columbia. Applicants must take and pass the North American Veterinary Licensing Exam, a 360-question multiple-choice test. They may also be required to take a state board exam and a test on the laws and regulations of the state where they intend to practice.

Many newly licensed veterinarians do a one-year internship to gain experience and improve their job prospects. Some doctors may join an existing practice or open one of their own. Still other veterinarians continue their training, perhaps by earning an advanced degree or becoming board certified in a specialty recognized by the AVMA. To become board certified, veterinarians must go through several steps. First, they choose from among the thirty-nine specialties recognized by the AVMA, such as avian (birds), equine, canine and feline, food animal, cardiology, nutrition, internal medicine, anesthesia, ophthalmology (eyes), and critical care. (Log on to the AVMA's website to see the full list.) Next, they study in a residency program for two to three years under the direction of board certified veterinarians in that specialty or at a university hospital. Finally, they must take and pass a written exam.

By the time a veterinarian's training is complete, he or she will have spent eight to twelve years in school. But an animal doctor's education never really ends. Veterinarians are required by law to take continuing education courses to renew their licenses every few years. Continuing education classes ensure doctors are up to date on the latest medical research, procedures, and advancements in the field. On their own, veterinarians read articles in professional journals, attend workshops, and meet with their peers. Their extensive training has taught them that when it comes to medicine, there is always something new to learn.

THREE

Veterinarians at Work

More than 80 percent of veterinarians in the United States work in private practice. These doctors may provide care for companion pets, exotic animals, or equines and large animals. Private practice veterinarians are similar to family doctors for humans. They treat animals with all kinds of injuries and illnesses, sometimes referring rare or difficult cases to specialists. Given that Americans love pets—we own nearly 165 million cats and dogs—veterinarians in private practice lead busy lives.

A veterinarian checks on his patients during morning rounds.

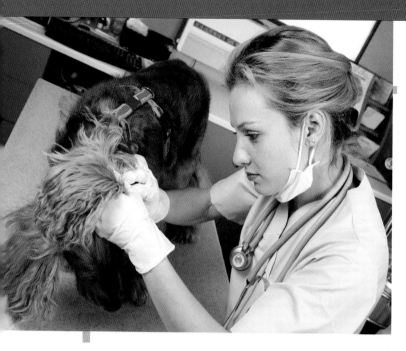

The Doctor Is In

For a veterinarian working in a small-animal clinic, the day begins with morning rounds. The doctor checks on the progress of the dogs, cats, and other animals in the kennel. In the reception area, veterinary assistants check in animals scheduled for surgery that day. A veterinary technician draws blood samples from the patients and performs lab tests to make sure the animals are healthy enough to handle anesthesia.

In the treatment area, the veterinarian prepares the first patient for surgery. The proper dose of anesthesia must be calculated and administered.

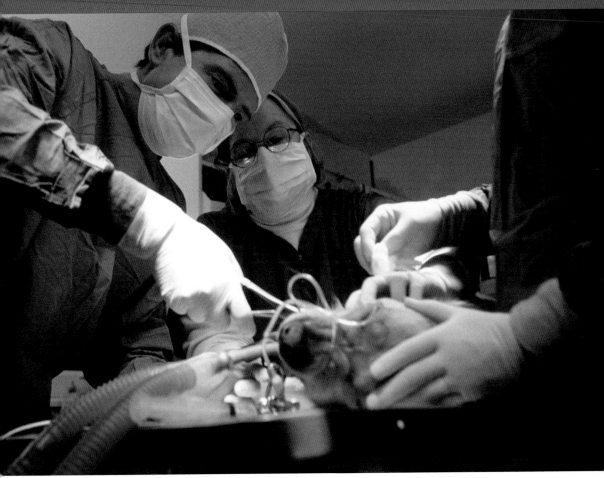

A veterinarian performs surgery while one technician assists and the other monitors the patient.

Once the animal is **anesthetized**, it's moved into a surgical suite, and the operation begins. Dental cleaning, tooth extraction, and spaying/neutering are the most common surgeries performed in a companion-animal practice. During each surgery, pulse rate, oxygen level, and other vital signs are carefully monitored by the veterinarian and his or her technicians. Once all of the morning surgeries are complete and the patients are in recovery, it's time for the veterinarian to move on to the day's scheduled appointments.

From late morning through the afternoon, a veterinarian sees numerous patients. New kittens and puppies come in for their first exams, vaccinations, and **microchips**. Cats and dogs arrive for routine wellness checkups. Animals that have previously had surgery return for follow-up care or to have their stitches removed. Ill animals arrive with infections or injuries. No matter how well-organized the day is, at any moment an animal with a life-threatening emergency may be brought through the doors. Things can quickly go from bustling to chaotic.

Working with any animal, even a dog or cat, carries risk. An animal that is frightened or in pain may lash out and scratch or bite the veterinarian trying to help it. Wounds may become infected or expose the doctor to an illness, such as cat scratch fever or rabies. Simply handling an infected animal may put a veterinarian at risk for salmonellosis or psittacosis (situh-KOH-sis), also known as parrot fever. Most of these diseases aren't fatal, but they

Tech Support

Veterinarians rely on receptionists, assistants, and technicians to keep the clinic running smoothly. A veterinary assistant usually has a high school diploma and trains on the job. Duties involve greeting clients, scheduling appointments, taking payments, and cleaning cages. A licensed veterinary technician, or LVT, is similar to a nurse. He or she gives medication to patients, draws blood, performs lab tests, takes and develops X-rays, and assists the veterinarian in surgery. An LVT may have either a two-year associate's degree or a four-year bachelor of science degree. Veterinary assistants earn about $22,000 per year, while LVTs earn between $30,000 and $40,000 a year.

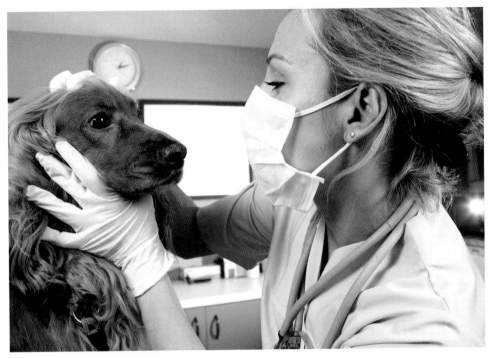

Protective gear, such as rubber gloves, provides a safe and clean working environment.

can be painful or uncomfortable. To help keep germs at bay, the veterinarian wears protective gear, such as a mask, gloves, and heavy clothing. The veterinarian frequently washes his or her hands and disinfects work areas and instruments.

Unlike a person, an animal can't explain where it hurts, so a veterinarian must be a bit like a detective. The doctor looks for clues about what could be causing the animal's illness. Does it have a fever? Is its coat smooth and shiny or rough and dull? Is a particular area of the body sensitive to touch? The veterinarian will also ask an owner questions. Has the animal's behavior changed recently? Has it gained or lost weight? Is it eating and drinking normally? To help with a **diagnosis**, laboratory work may be ordered, such as blood, urine, or **fecal** tests. X-rays or an **ultrasound** may also be useful. Once the doctor has a diagnosis, he or she prescribes a course of treatment. This may involve medication, a dietary change, physical therapy, more tests, or a referral to a specialist.

By late afternoon, most surgery patients are on their way home. For those staying overnight, the veterinarian contacts each owner with a progress report. The doctor also reviews lab and test results, writes notes in medical records, returns phone calls, and handles business matters. It's a long day—sometimes stretching to twelve hours or more. And the next day, the cycle starts all over again.

A Woman's Place Is In the... Barn!

At one time, veterinary medicine was for men only. It was thought that women were too fragile to handle large animals. To gain entrance into the profession, women had to prove they were just as smart, dedicated, and strong as men. The U.S. Census reported that in 1960, only 2 percent of veterinarians were female. The civil rights movement of the 1960s and 1972's Title IX law, which prohibited discrimination in education, helped turn the tide. Today, more than half the veterinarians in the United States are women, and in veterinary schools, females outnumber males by three to one!

Veterinarians on the Go

About one-quarter of veterinarians in private practice specialize in treating equines, large animals, or a combination of the two. It's much easier for the veterinarian to visit the barn than it is to bring a large, lumbering animal into a clinic. This is known as **ambulatory medicine**.

A large-animal or equine ambulatory veterinarian typically drives a vehicle that is fully stocked to handle everything from routine procedures to serious emergencies. A truck may have its own pharmacy and laboratory, as well as radiology and ultrasound equipment. An ambulatory doctor in a rural area may cover hundreds of miles each week, providing health care to horses, cattle, sheep, and other livestock on farms and ranches.

Livestock on a farm receive the same kind of attention smaller animals get in an office setting. A veterinarian gives health exams, dental care, and vaccinations. He or she may treat wounds, set broken bones, test for diseases, perform surgery, and assist animals that are giving birth. The doctor also consults with owners on the topics of nutrition, breeding, and housing. Additionally, people considering buying a horse or large animal have a veterinarian come out to do a prepurchase physical and lameness exam to be sure the animal they want to buy is healthy.

Large-animal veterinarians just out of school earn about $70,000 a year, while those with more experience earn $90,000 or more per year. Equine veterinarians generally earn less than their counterparts who treat companion and large animals. Annual salaries for them begin at about $50,000, with the average being around $70,000.

Although most veterinarians opt for private practice, this is only one corner of veterinary medicine. Keep reading to discover the many ways veterinarians contribute to the well-being of not just animals but people, too.

Large-animal veterinarians examine and treat their patients on farms and ranches.

FOUR

Explore Your Options

From saving wildlife to searching for the newest wonder drug, those who pursue a career in veterinary medicine have many paths from which to choose. About 20 percent of veterinarians in the United States are employed by businesses, nonprofit groups, government agencies, or colleges and universities. Most of these 18,000 veterinarians care for animals, but others are responsible for the health and safety of the public. This chapter will give you a closer look at some different types of veterinarians and what to do to prepare for a career in each area.

It's a Jungle Out There

Imagine performing an ultrasound exam on a python or cleaning an armadillo's teeth. It's what veterinarians who work with animals in zoos and aquariums do every day. A zoo-animal or marine veterinarian may be responsible for the health care of hundreds, even thousands, of different animals, from kiwi birds to African elephants.

For creatures that would normally be prey in the wild, showing signs of illness indicates weakness. Frequently, the first and only sign that an animal is having a health issue is a slight change in behavior. This is why zoo-animal veterinarians must be good observers. They need to be able to work in tandem with zookeepers and animal handlers to spot health issues early on. A zoo-

Zoo veterinarians examine and treat the wide variety of animals that live at zoos.

animal veterinarian's duties include collecting blood and urine samples, giving vaccines, treating illness and injury, and doing routine health exams. Zoo-animal veterinarians also perform surgery, give postoperative care, provide nutritional advice to keepers, and oversee breeding programs.

There are only about four hundred zoos and aquariums in the United States, so the job market in this area is extremely competitive. Those who want to work in the field should get as much hands-on experience as they can with wildlife, starting as early as possible. Middle school or high school students should volunteer at a veterinary clinic, farm, or wildlife sanctuary. At school, they should take courses in biology, zoology, and animal science. College students are advised to take courses in zoology, biology, genetics, and marine and animal science. In veterinary school, students should do an externship at a zoo, aquarium, wildlife center, or scientific research facility. After college, it's recommended that veterinarians become board certified in zoological medicine and do their residency at a zoo or aquarium. This will help increase their chances of getting hired.

A Valuable Veterinarian

In the summer of 1999, several senior citizens in New York City became seriously ill. At the same time, crows in the city began dying. After initial tests, public health experts announced the birds and humans had been infected with the virus that causes St. Louis encephalitis, a disease that causes brain swelling. But Dr. Tracey McNamara, senior **pathologist** at the Bronx Zoo, thought something else might be going on. The veterinarian pressed the government to do further testing. Dr. McNamara sent tissue samples from some of the zoo's dead birds to government labs, and the true culprit was found: West Nile virus. Spread by mosquitoes, West Nile virus had originally been discovered in Africa in the 1930s, but the disease had never been seen in the United States. Within three years, the zoonotic disease found its way into almost every state in the nation. (Most people who are infected don't get seriously ill.) For her extraordinary efforts, Dr. McNamara received the AVMA's highest award.

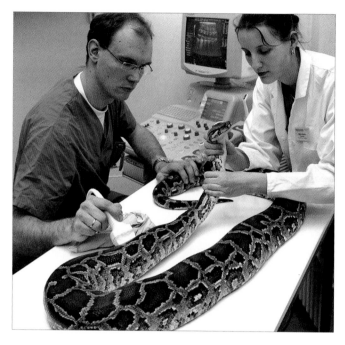

A wildlife veterinarian examines a python at the wildlife clinic at Tufts University School of Veterinary Medicine in Massachusetts.

The competition for jobs in zoos and aquariums may be steep, but fortunately, more options exist for working with wildlife. National parks, rehabilitation centers, and sanctuaries also employ veterinarians with a zoological medicine specialty. Wildlife veterinarians generally help animals that are sick or injured. They may treat songbirds, raptors, deer, raccoons, bobcats, or marine mammals. Frequently, the goal is to nurse the animal back to health and return it to its natural habitat. Some veterinarians work alongside biologists, who study and monitor wildlife. Biologists track the habits, migration patterns, and populations of fish, waterfowl, raptors, wolves, cougars, bears, and other wild animals. When working in the field, a veterinarian is responsible for sedating an animal, giving it a brief health exam, treating any injuries, collecting a blood sample, and tagging it for future tracking. He or she may also record information about the animal, like measuring body size and inspecting its teeth to determine its approximate age.

Sometimes, an animal must be relocated to help reintroduce a species to a particular area. A wildlife veterinarian will sedate the animal and monitor its vital signs during transport. In all cases of capture, a veterinarian is responsible for reviving the animal and helping to ensure its safe release. Wildlife veterinarians may also act as investigators, performing tests on dead animals to discover the cause of death. Their work is often instrumental in saving wildlife populations from being wiped out by disease, pollution, predators, or other dangers. To work as a wildlife veterinarian, students should take the same classes and get the same experience as they would to work in a zoo or aquarium. The yearly salaries of zoo and wildlife veterinarians vary widely, from $60,000 to $140,000, depending on the location, type, and size of the employer.

Looking Out for Us

Veterinarians not only care for animals, they protect the public, too. Numerous city, county, and state governments, along with federal agencies, employ veterinarians in the area of **epidemiology.** Their job is to study, prevent, and manage outbreaks of infectious diseases.

More than 3,000 veterinarians work for the U.S. government to keep food, water, and the environment free of harmful bacteria and disease. Over half of those are employed by the U.S. Department of Agriculture. Some veterinarians inspect livestock, poultry, fish, and other animals that are headed for the food supply. Others oversee processing plants, restaurants, and water reservoirs. Veterinarians also check animal products coming into and leaving the country to make sure they are disease-free. Some veterinarians inspect and **quarantine** live animals brought into the United States from foreign countries. They test for diseases, oversee the interstate shipment of animals, and educate the public on infectious diseases. Veterinarians at the

U.S. Food and Drug Administration test medications, medical products, food additives, and pet foods. At the Environmental Protection Agency, veterinarians study the impact of pollutants, pesticides, and other chemicals on people and animals. Nearly one hundred veterinarians work for the Centers for Disease Control and Prevention (CDC) in Atlanta, Georgia, an organization that studies diseases, monitors public health, and develops programs to prevent the spread of disease. Veterinary epidemiologists at the CDC research zoonotic diseases such as West Nile virus, Ebola, monkeypox, and avian flu. They also investigate diseases that could be used in bioterrorism, the deliberate release of bacteria and viruses intended to cause harm. These include smallpox, anthrax, hantavirus, and cholera.

Veterinarians with the Department of Homeland Security (DHS) are trained to respond to emergency situations that put the health of people and animals at risk. In the event of a catastrophe, such as a major disease epidemic, natural disaster, or bioterrorist attack, DHS veterinarians coordinate efforts to contain the threat, rescue animals, and protect the public. Similarly, veterinarians in the armed forces also focus their efforts on public safety. The U.S. Air Force Biomedical Science Corps manages communicable disease programs and works as a public health service. The U.S. Army Veterinary Corps researches bioterrorist technologies and develops strategies to prevent and prepare for possible attacks.

Veterinary students who want a career in public health and safety should do an externship in the area in which they want to work, perhaps with their state health department or with a government agency such as the USDA or CDC. For those interested in homeland security, the U.S. Navy offers an externship with its Marine Mammal Program in San Diego, California. It's an opportunity for fourth-year veterinary students to help care for the dolphins and sea lions used in underwater mine and weapons detection.

Veterinarians may improve their odds of being hired by completing studies in epidemiology, virology (viruses), pathology (diseases), beef cattle practice, or food-animal practice. They should then do residency training or graduate studies to obtain a master's degree or doctorate (PhD). Many do both, enrolling in a combined residency and PhD program. Veterinarians employed in food safety, public health, and homeland security can expect to earn between $70,000 and $95,000 a year.

The Navy's Marine Mammal Program offers externships for veterinary students interested in a career in public health and safety.

Serving Country and Canine

Since 1916 the U.S. Army Veterinary Corps has been protecting the animals that have been protecting us. Veterinarians in the armed services provide health care for military working dogs, mine-detecting dolphins and sea lions, therapy animals, and soldiers' pets. There are more than 2,700 military working dogs on duty around the world, chasing down criminals, protecting troops, and sniffing out drugs, explosives, and weapons. When these four-footed canine soldiers get sick or injured, they may be treated in the field or **medevaced** to the one-of-a-kind Holland Military Working Dog Hospital at Lackland Air Force Base in San Antonio, Texas. Currently, about seven hundred veterinarians serve on active duty and in the reserves with the Veterinary Corps, which is also responsible for inspecting all of the food and water supplied to American troops serving overseas. Salary is determined by rank and experience, ranging from $67,000 to $97,000 a year.

Breaking New Ground

Another field that offers growing potential for veterinarians is **biomedical research**. Working in a laboratory, a research veterinarian may conduct health studies or develop drugs, antibiotics, vaccines, or other medical treatments. Typically, the government, universities, medical organizations, and private companies employ research veterinarians.

According to the AVMA, much of the progress made in human and animal medicine in the United States over the course of the last century would not have been possible without the veterinarians in the biomedical field. Thanks to their work, we know more about, and are able to treat, illnesses such as botulism, malaria, and yellow fever. Veterinarians have also made advances in the areas of organ transplants, artificial limbs, and joint and heart disease. They know the surgical techniques they perfect today on animals will likely one day benefit humans. Research veterinarians usually specialize in pharmacology (drugs), toxicology (poisons), virology, pathology, or laboratory-animal medicine. Frequently, they have an advanced degree, such as a master's degree or a PhD. In terms of salary, veterinarians who work in research are in the top 10 percent of earners in their field, making more than $143,000 per year.

Whether setting a fawn's broken leg or peering into a microscope, a veterinarian's first duty is to respect life. No matter where the road leads, the oath taken by every veterinarian is an ever-present reminder of personal responsibility and public trust. As you are about to discover, it is a vow not taken lightly.

FIVE

Meet The Veterinarians

When Dr. Stephanie Meyer's phone rings at two o'clock in the morning, it's almost a certainty there's going to be a worried horse owner on the other end. As the head of an ambulatory equine unit for a small- and large-animal private practice, Dr. Meyer is used to rolling out of bed at all hours to handle emergencies. She doesn't mind. In fact, she lives for it. "What I do can be a hard, physical job," she says. "But there's a great amount of satisfaction that goes with it. I love the freedom of being outside. And I like working under pressure. It's an adrenaline rush."

Day or night, in all kinds of weather, Dr. Meyer may travel up to fifty miles to tend to her equine patients. Her truck is fully stocked with medication, supplies, and surgical tools. She must be prepared for anything. Most of her emergency calls involve lameness, cuts, puncture wounds, colic (a potentially life threatening digestive blockage), or a horse who is having trouble giving birth. "Horses aren't that much different than people when it comes to their personalities," she says. "Each one is different. There are differences in the breeds, too. I'm not a very big person, but size isn't the issue when you work with horses. It's all about knowing how to approach the animal and moving safely around them."

Dr. Meyer has owned and adored horses since she was a child, so there was never any doubt in her mind that she would one day work on their behalf. But the Texas A&M University College of Veterinary Medicine

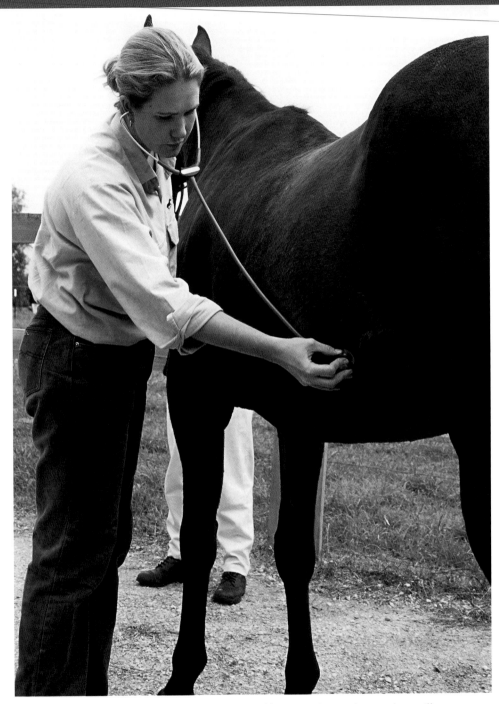

This veterinarian specializes in equine care. She examines a horse that will compete in the Grand National Rodeo.

The Changing Face of Medicine

Once reserved only for humans, treatments such as **acupuncture**, massage, and chiropractic are now benefiting animals, too. When her own horse had a medical issue that Western medicine couldn't solve, Dr. Meyer found the answer in Chinese herbs and acupuncture. She then studied to become a certified veterinary acupuncturist. Today, Dr. Meyer leads a team that practices integrative medicine. They use a combination of Western and traditional Chinese medicine to treat cats, dogs, horses, and even alpacas. She says horses can become so relaxed during acupuncture that they fall asleep during the painless procedure of inserting small needles into pressure points on the body. Acupuncture and herbs are effective in helping animals with arthritis, back and joint pain, skin problems, and cancer.

graduate says having a passion for animals is only a small part of the job. "Most people don't realize that working with animals is really about one third of what we do," she explains. "The other two-thirds is working with the animal owner: educating them, advising them, comforting them. You have to be a people person. When you are standing outside in the freezing cold in the middle of the night and an animal owner is figuring out what he wants to do, well, then you stand there for as long as it takes for him to make that decision. Your job is to help that person with whatever they are going through with their animal. That's why I love it. I love helping."

Good communication skills are needed in order to educate, advise, and comfort pet owners.

A Good Bedside Manner

Many people think working with animals means you don't have to deal with people. This couldn't be further from the truth. It's essential for a veterinarian to be a people person, because pets have owners. A veterinarian has to have excellent communication skills and the ability to explain complex medical terms in a simple way. A veterinarian must be a good listener, too. Owners should feel free to ask questions, express concerns, and offer input. Also, a doctor must be calm. Having a sick or injured pet is stressful. It's not uncommon for owners to be indecisive, scared, or even angry. Certainly, nothing is more challenging than when owners must make the difficult decision to have the veterinarian **euthanize** a pet. Those going through the heartbreak of loss appreciate a doctor who is gentle and comforting.

There's a Wallaby in the Lobby

At the Avian and Exotic Clinic of the Monterey Peninsula in California, Dr. Shannon Thomas trims the nails of her first three patients: a **budgie**, a lovebird, and a rabbit. She examines an iguana that's not eating well and is dragging a leg. Next comes a rabbit with balance problems, likely due to a parasite (she'll know more when she sees the results from the blood tests). The rabbit is followed by an emergency—a lovebird that was stepped on accidentally by its owner. And it's not yet noon.

From hedgehogs to bearded dragons to California condors, if it crawls, slithers, waddles, hops, or flies, it's a good bet Dr. Thomas has probably treated it. "You never know what is going to come through the doors on any given day," she says. "Last week, we had a wallaby come in from the local animal park."

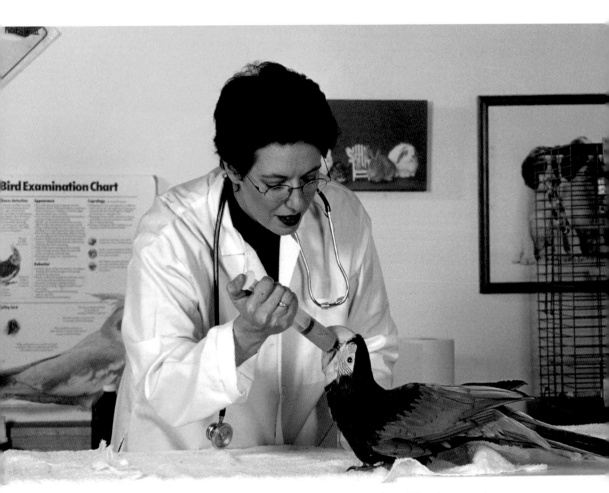

A veterinarian specializing in avian veterinary medicine hand feeds an eighteen-week-old green-winged macaw.

Growing up on the Monterey Peninsula, Dr. Thomas knew she wanted a career with animals almost before she could read. As a child, she was always tending injured birds and small wildlife. While in veterinary school, she kept a pet iguana and birds. When she realized she knew more about caring for them than many professionals did, she decided to make exotics her specialty. Her passion for animals becomes clear when you find out just how many pets she has now: an African tortoise, a python, a chinchilla, a dog, a cat, two ducks, two donkeys, two horses, three rabbits, a senegal, three macaws, fourteen chickens, "and a gecko running loose in the house."

Dr. Thomas says one of the perks of working with exotics and wildlife is that she is always learning. If she doesn't have the answer for a particular health issue, she knows she can turn to her peers for help, and vice versa. In the case of the wallaby (he had a gastrointestinal infection), she called colleagues in Australia for advice.

Of the many animals she treats, Dr. Thomas has a soft spot for birds. "Birds may seem fragile, but they are tougher than you think," she says. And what about this morning's emergency, the lovebird who got trampled underfoot? "He's breathing a little heavily, so he might have a lung **contusion**," she says. "But he should pull through."

SIX

Peer into the Future

What will the job market be like for veterinarians in the years to come? Most sources say the outlook is quite good. The U.S. Bureau of Labor Statistics reports that veterinarian employment is expected to increase by more than 30 percent between 2008 and 2018, meaning another 30,000 veterinarians will be needed before the decade is out. This is a much faster growth rate than the average for all other occupations.

But not everyone sees such a rosy picture. A 2011 study by the AVMA found that recent graduates from veterinary schools were getting fewer job offers and earning less in their first year of practice. In 2008 the survey found graduating seniors had received, on average, 2.5 job offers. That dropped to 1.6 job offers in 2011.

Another challenge is balancing the high cost of veterinary school with fulfilling a dream. Statistics show the average veterinary student graduates with about $140,000 of student loan debt. There is concern that as the cost of education rises and salaries fall, many who wish to pursue veterinary medicine won't be able to afford it. "While that debt is high and concerning to us all, there are lots of repayment options that can help students retire their debt," says Lisa Greenhill of the AAVMC.

Debate also surrounds the types of veterinarians that will be most in demand in the future. According to the AVMA, there is currently a shortage

Animal CSI

Forensic medicine is a fairly young but rapidly growing area of veterinary science. Forensic veterinarians assist law enforcement in investigating incidents of animal abuse and neglect. In cases where animals have died as a result of criminal activity, veterinarians process crime scene information and work with the legal system to bring criminals to justice. They also educate the public on animal hoarding, puppy mills, and other types of animal cruelty.

of large-animal, or food-supply, veterinarians. The association says the situation will only get worse, growing by 2 to 4 percent each year. It may even put America's food supply at risk. The USDA recently started a program to offset the shortage. Veterinarians who agree to practice in designated shortage areas for three years after graduation may have up to $75,000 of their educational

Today, there is a need for large animal/food supply veterinarians.

debt paid by the government. Yet, a recent report by a committee from the American Association of Bovine Practitioners (AABP) found there was no crisis. Instead, the group cited the downturn in the economy as the main reason for the lack of large-animal veterinarian practices in rural areas. Big losses in the dairy, cattle, and agriculture industries have meant some small communities simply aren't able to sustain large-animal practices. The AABP says there are more large animal veterinarians than available jobs, and "creating an over-supply of food supply veterinarians will lead to widespread unemployment."

Most experts do agree that certain areas of veterinary medicine will offer more career potential than others in the coming years. These include

- food and water safety
- food-animal welfare and inspection
- animal welfare (forensic medicine)
- biomedical research
- bioterrorism and homeland security

Employers most likely to be hiring include private research facilities, pharmaceutical companies, and agencies within the U.S. government such as the USDA, the CDC, the DHS, and the armed forces.

Caring for Fluffy and Fido

With 70 percent of new graduates from US veterinary schools choosing to go into companion-animal care, there is concern that the United States may end up with far more dog and cat veterinarians than we need. Even so, the U.S. Department of Labor says that pet ownership will continue to grow steadily, and with it, the need for veterinarians. Cat care is expected to experience the most dramatic increase.

More than 70 million people own pets. Healthcare for these pets, along with large and exotic animals, is much needed.

Statistics show more than 60 percent of American households have pets. In 2011 Americans spent $14 billion on veterinary care for their pets—over $1 billion more than the previous year. Pet owners are becoming more educated about preventive care, such as regular checkups, dental cleanings, and vaccinations. Many are choosing advanced care, too, like cancer treatments, physical therapy, and joint replacements. Also, more are opting for alternative medicine, such as massage, herbal therapy, and acupuncture, either alone or in combination with standard Western medicine.

Like health care for humans, the face of veterinary medical care is changing. Twenty-five years ago, private practice veterinarians referred only their most extreme cases to specialists, who could be found only at university

Rescue Me

The millions of companion animals brought to city, county, and private animal shelters in the United States each year are cared for by veterinarians. Shelter veterinarians treat injuries and illnesses, provide vaccinations, implant microchips, and spay and neuter animals. Many shelters are no-kill facilities, meaning they do not euthanize healthy pets, but others are not. Because of growth and interest within the field, the AVMA is currently considering adding shelter medicine to its list of board specialties. Depending on experience and a shelter's size and location, a shelter veterinarian can earn between $50,000 and $90,000 per year. To learn more, visit the Association of Shelter Veterinarians website.

teaching hospitals. Today, specialists are no longer limited to a university setting. Many have their own private practices. This allows companion-animal veterinarians to act as primary care providers, referring patients with specific health issues to them for care. Such a partnership is beneficial to everyone. It increases a pet's life span, creates a strong client-doctor relationship, and allows a veterinary practice to grow. Experts predict that in the future, more veterinary specialists will be needed in areas like nutrition, dentistry, surgery, and oncology (cancer).

Along with finding their niche in medicine, companion animal veterinaians must also be skilled in business and marketing. A veterinarian starting his or her own practice will spend more than $300,000 in start-up costs. Expenses include leasing office space, purchasing equipment and furniture, and hiring a staff. Teaming up with other animal doctors or buying an existing practice can reduce costs. Another option is to have a non-veterinary business partner (this is not allowed in every state, so you'll need to check the laws in your state). A website, advertising, and other promotional efforts are also key components of a sustainable veterinary practice.

Experts say the way veterinarians do business is also undergoing a shift. A struggling economy and rising veterinary costs are impacting how pet owners choose to provide care for their animals. Rather than going to a traditional veterinary clinic, some pet owners are opting for low-cost spay/neuter and vaccination clinics. Others are turning to web-based sources for information on pet illnesses or injuries (diagnosing a pet yourself is never a good idea). "For companion animal practitioners, economic challenges always have been among the toughest challenges facing veterinarians," says Sharon Curtis Granskog of the American Veterinary Medical Association. "No matter how strong the human animal bond, treatment of companion animals is generally considered in the realm of discretionary income." To reach out

Taking Care of Yourself

Veterinarians tend to be sensitive, caring, and hardworking—all good qualities to have unless someone is working too many hours or under too much stress. Then the emotional toll of tending to ill animals and their owners can lead to burn-out, or what is called compassion fatigue. Dr. Lisa Miller, former chair of the AVMA Committee on Wellness, says it's important for veterinarians to make physical and mental health a priority. She advises veterinarians to eat right, exercise, get plenty of sleep, utilize relaxation techniques, spend time with family and friends, and engage in fun activities.

to clients, veterinarians are offering competitive pricing and more affordable payment plans. They feature up-to-date websites with reliable information, as well as online pet records and appointments. They are extending their office hours to include evenings and weekends. Some veterinarians even make house calls. Experts say this kind of innovation in the industry is what will help the next generation of veterinarians find success in the marketplace.

As you've seen, the path to becoming, and remaining, a veterinarian can be challenging. Yet, with preparation, training, determination, and passion it is an achievable goal that results in a satisfying profession. For as long as there are animals to care for, owners to soothe, people to protect, and new discoveries to be made, there will always be a place in the world for veterinarians.

Glossary

acupuncture	the traditional Chinese medical practice of inserting small needles just under the skin at various points of the body to treat illness and pain
ambulatory medicine	on-site veterinary care, often provided for horses, livestock, and other large animals
anatomy	the scientific study of the structure of animals and plants
anesthesia	drugs administered to bring about insensitivity or unconsciousness
anesthetized	to be rendered insensitive or unconscious through the administration of drugs
biomedical research	the laboratory study of diseases, treatments, and cures
budgie	short for budgerigar, a type of Australian parakeet
canine	pertaining to dogs
contusion	a bruise
diagnosis	the determination of a cause of an illness or injury through medical examination
epidemiology	the study of what causes outbreaks of infectious diseases
euthanize	to humanely put an animal to death to relieve its pain and suffering
externship	an off-campus, supervised work-experience program for college students

fecal	pertaining to waste matter discharged from the intestines
feline	pertaining to cats
internship	a paid or volunteer work-experience program in a professional workplace
livestock	horses, cattle, sheep, and other farm animals
medevac	short for "medical evacuation," the transportation of the sick or injured via ambulance or helicopter to a medical facility for treatment
microchips	tiny integrated circuits implanted under the skin of cats and dogs that, when scanned, provide identification information
quarantine	to enforce a period of strict isolation to prevent the spread of an infectious disease
pathologist	someone who studies the origin, nature, and course of diseases
residency	a two- to three-year program in which a veterinarian gains advanced training in a specialty area
ultrasound	the use of sound waves to create internal images of the body
undergraduate	a college student who has not yet received a four-year degree
wildlife sanctuary	a protected area, location, or facility for animals

Find Out More

Books

Field, Shelly. *Career Opportunities: Working with Animals*. New York: Checkmark Books, 2012.

Hollow, Michele C. and William P. Rives. *The Everything Guide to Working with Animals*. Avon, MA: Adams Media, 2010.

Lee, Mary Price and Richard S. Lee. *Opportunities in Animal and Pet Care Careers*. New York: McGraw Hill, 2009.

Ryan-Flynn, Mary Susan. *What Can I Do Now? Animal Careers*. New York: Ferguson, 2010.

Websites

American Association of Zoo Veterinarians

www.aazv.org

Log on to learn about career opportunities as a zoo or aquarium veterinarian. Find scholarships, externships, internships, and pre-veterinary clubs.

American Veterinary Medical Association (AVMA)

www.avma.org

The AVMA is the leading veterinary professional organization in the United States. On its website, you can view a complete list of veterinary specialties, get tips on preparing for veterinary school, and download posters and curriculum materials. Click on the video links to see veterinarians at work.

Association of American Veterinary Medical Colleges (AAVMC)

www.aavmc.org

The AAVMC has a complete list of national and international accredited veterinary colleges, along with descriptor pages that explain prerequisites and application requirements for most of them. You can also explore careers in veterinary medicine, find preveterinary resources, and learn more about the veterinary school application process.

Index

educational requirements,
    13-16, 33, 34
getting licensed, 22
history of, 7, **7**
job market, 48-55
origin of name, 7
specialties, 23
typical day, 4, **5**, 25, 26, 30
working with people, 45
veterinarian's oath, **22**
veterinary school, 11-15, 34
virology, 40
VMCAs, 17
volunteering, 12, 33

West Nile virus, 37
wildlife sanctuaries, 10, 35
wildlife veterinarians, 35
women in veterinary medicine, 29

zoo veterinarians, 32-36, **33**
zoonotic diseases, 10, 34
zoos, 10, 32-35

About the Author

Trudi Strain Trueit is the author of more than eighty fiction and nonfiction books for young readers. A former television journalist and weather forecaster, she enjoys writing about career exploration, health, weather, earth science, and history. Look for her other titles in the Careers with Animals series: *Animal Physical Therapist*, *Animal Trainer*, and *Wildlife Conservationist*. Trueit has a bachelor's degree in broadcast journalism and lives in Everett, Washington, with her husband and their two cats. Read more about Trueit and her books at www.truditrueit.com.